BURIED
....
TREASURE
....

First published in 2025 by the National Maritime Museum, Park Row,
Greenwich, London SE10 9NF. publishing@rmg.co.uk

ISBN: 978-1-7391542-8-8

Inspired by the *Pirates* exhibition originally co-produced by the
National Maritime Museum Cornwall and the National Maritime
Museum, Greenwich, London, with consultant curator Dr Eric Kentley.
Text © National Maritime Museum, Greenwich, London.

At the heart of the UNESCO World Heritage Site of Maritime Greenwich
are the four world-class attractions of Royal Museums Greenwich – the
National Maritime Museum, the Royal Observatory, the Queen's House
and *Cutty Sark*.

rmg.co.uk

All rights reserved. No part of this publication may be reproduced,
stored in or introduced into a retrieval system, or transmitted in any
form, or by any means (electronic, mechanical, photocopying, recording
or otherwise) without the prior written permission of the publisher. Any
person who commits any unauthorised act in relation to this publication
may be liable to criminal prosecution and civil claims for damages.

A CIP catalogue record for this book is available from the British Library.

Image credits: Cover: skull, parrot, barrel, treasure chest, compass, flag
public domain CC0 images, courtesy of Rawpixel; pages 18, 23, 42, 54,
55, 56, 58, 66, 71, 99, 101, 122 © National Maritime Museum, Greenwich,
London. All other images courtesy of stock.adobe.com

Cover and series design concept by Matt Windsor
Design and typesetting by seagulls.net
Printed and bound in Slovenia by DZS Grafik

10 9 8 7 6 5 4 3 2 1

BURIED
TREASURE

A Pirate Miscellany

*In memory of our friend and colleague
Dr Robert Blyth, who had a gift for
storytelling and shared his knowledge
generously with all who knew him.*

PIRATE PARLANCE

....

Before entering the murky and
murderous world of pirates we should
begin with the boring but necessary
task of defining some basic terms
to avoid confusion and chaos…

Piracy, *n.* robbery on the seas

Pirate, *n.* a person who commits piracy

Privateer, 1. *n.* an armed vessel owned and crewed by private individuals with a government commission to capture the merchant shipping of an enemy nation 2. *n.* an individual holding such a commission

The first two definitions should be straightforward. The third is a bit more complicated, but pirates and piracy are the focus here. The legalistic peculiarities of privateers and privateering will be mentioned only occasionally – promise!

WHY IS THIS BOOK CALLED *BURIED TREASURE?*

This is wrong, wrong, wrong! Pirates almost never buried their treasure. They mainly spent it quickly. Pirates also didn't make secret maps to help find buried treasure. So why do we think they did? It's all the fault of fiction. In books like Robert Louis Stevenson's (1850–94) *Treasure Island*, maps where X marks the spot of a hidden hoard of gold, silver and precious jewels are a key part of the adventurous plots.

Now, it must be admitted that Captain William Kidd did bury some treasure once, but just once. This was hidden on Gardiner's Island, near Long Island, New York in 1699. It remains unclear how much treasure he buried. At least some of it was uncovered and sent to London as evidence at his trial for piracy and murder. Despite many searches, nothing else has yet been found. Presumably Kidd expected to recall where he'd stashed the valuables, so he probably felt no need to draw a map.

But there is, of course, plenty of pirate treasure buried within this useful little book. So, get digging to discover some piratical gems of a miscellaneous, mischievous and largely truthful nature...

WHEN DID PIRACY BEGIN?

There is no precise date. The main definition of piracy is robbery on the seas. This means that piracy began as soon as humans started moving things by sea that others thought worth stealing. So, pirates have been around for at least several thousand years and are still with us today.

Some writers like to refer to the 'golden age' of piracy, but what does this mean? Well, it was a period of considerable pirate activity between roughly the 1680s and the 1720s. Many of the most famous pirates of the Western world – Blackbeard,

Captain Kidd, Henry Every, Bartholomew Roberts and many others – were around at this time.

Pirates were stealing from ships in the Caribbean, along the east coast of North America, off the West African coast and in the Indian Ocean. This caused major problems for trade. They became the scourge of the high seas and a menace that governments had to deal with. During the 1720s, pirates were increasingly hunted down, bringing the 'golden age' to an end.

> **RASCALLY REALITY**
> *Sailors from captured ships often joined the pirate crew. As they saw stolen goods and money fairly distributed among the pirates, they were tempted by the prospect of quick riches and what they thought might be an easier life.*

PIRATES IN THE PRESS

Pirate adventures and courtroom trials made good press stories. They featured regularly in early eighteenth-century newspapers and helped shift copies to a public keen to learn the grisly details of the latest pirate heist or the most recent death sentences. But journalists and editors also exaggerated the stories to make pirates appear even more violent and destructive. The 'golden age of piracy' was no stranger to fake news!

Corsairs' Chronicle

14 APRIL 1720 — 1 piece of eight

PLUNDERING PIRATES POSE PESKY PROBLEM

By all our letters from the Coast of Guinea, from Carolina, from Barbados, from Jamaica, etc. they [pirates] behave now with an unparalleled insolence, and appear more numerous and powerful than ever was known. They add that they have plundered and burnt at least forty ships belonging only to the Port of London and Bristol [...] and seem to defy any attempts that may be made to destroy them.

From the *Weekly Journal; or Saturday's Post*, 14 April 1720*

---

* The *Corsairs' Chronicle*, *Buccaneers' Bugle*, *Piratical Post* and the headlines represented in this book are works of fiction, but their reports from the dark days of the pirate past are real.

WILLIAM KIDD

> BORN: *Greenock or Dundee, Scotland, about 1645*
> PIRATE CAREER: *1697–99*
> DIED: *hanged, Execution Dock, London, England, 23 May 1701*

Captain William Kidd began his career as a privateer, hunting pirates on behalf of the government with his ship the *Adventure Galley*. But the pirate hunter soon became a wanted pirate. On 30 January 1698, he captured the *Quedagh Merchant*, an Indian ship carrying gold, silver and valuable textiles, making his fortune. Kidd kept the ship, renaming it the *Adventure Prize*. But his success as a pirate came at a cost – he was now a wanted man.

He was arrested in New York in June 1699 and then sent to London for trial. But Kidd was not tried immediately and spent many months locked up in terrible conditions in Newgate Prison. He assumed his political connections, carefully cultivated when he was a privateer, would secure him a pardon. But Kidd's luck had run out. He was eventually found guilty of piracy and murder, having killed one of his crew, William Moore, by fracturing his skull with a bucket. Kidd was sentenced to death.

AND DID HIS HANGING GO SMOOTHLY?

No, it didn't! Kidd was sent to be hanged at Execution Dock at Wapping on the banks of the River Thames on 23 May 1701. When the chaplain attended Kidd before the execution, he found him drunk. It was quite usual for the condemned criminal to be given a final drink, but Kidd seems to have had several. The hangman placed the rope around Kidd's neck, but it snapped, and he fell to the ground uninjured. Some of the crowd who had gathered to see the execution thought it was an act of God and a sign of Kidd's innocence. There were shouts for him to be released. However, a new length of rope was produced. This time there was no escape for the notorious Captain Kidd.

His dead body was later put in an iron gibbet cage and hung up at Tilbury Point in Essex.

It remained there on public view for three years as a warning to would-be pirates who wanted to follow in his footsteps.

Buccaneers' Bugle

13 APRIL 1700 — 1 piece of eight

CAPTAIN KIDD CUFFED IN CLINK

On Sunday last the famous pirate Capt. Kidd was brought prisoner under a strong guard to the Admiralty Office, where the Lords of the Admiralty examined him, and about 10 a clock at night he was carried to Newgate; he was in irons and had handcuffs. Fourteen more of his crew are brought in a yacht to Greenwich, being all in irons, and one of them has handcuffs.

From *The Post Boy*, 13 April 1700

BARTHOLOMEW ROBERTS

> **Born:** *Casnewydd-Bach, Wales, about 1682*
> **Pirate career:** *1719–22*
> **Died:** *killed in battle, 10 February 1722*

In 1719, Bartholomew Roberts was third in command of a slave ship when it was captured by pirates. He was forced to join the crew of Howell Davis, a fellow Welshman. Roberts soon saw piracy's potential. After Davis was shot dead, Roberts became the pirate captain.

He became a most successful pirate and was known as 'Black Bart'. He captured several hundred vessels, mainly around the Caribbean and North America. In 1722, while raiding ships off the west coast of Africa, Roberts was intercepted by Captain Chaloner Ogle of the Royal Navy. In the battle that followed, Roberts was killed.

POLLY ROGER, THE PIRATE PARROT

Polly Roger began her pirate career as a fledgling (literally). She has pirated around the globe, avoiding capture by taking flight (literally) at the first sight of the forces of law and order. During her travels and adventures, Polly has developed a deep knowledge of piratical terminology, making her the wise old bird (literally) of the pirate world. If you want to learn how to speak (or squawk) like a pirate, let Polly take you under her wing (literally) for a master class…

BORN: *no, hatched*
PIRATE CAREER: *ongoing*
DIED: *not yet, cheeky!*

LESSON 1

....

BUCCANEERING BASICS FOR BEGINNERS, OR GETTING STARTED WITH PIRATE-SPEAK

Doctors talk like doctors, using words we sometimes don't understand. Lawyers talk like lawyers, using words we almost never understand. And, of course, pirates talk like pirates, using their own words and phrases. Polly Roger will be your guide:

Go on account: become a pirate

Freebooter: a Dutch word for a pirate

Filibuster: a Spanish word for a pirate

Corsair: a French word for a pirate, especially one from North Africa

Jolly Roger: a pirate flag

'Aaargh! It's the Jolly Roger – it's a pirate ship.'

FEATHERY FACT

Pirates may have had parrots, but probably as valuable things to sell rather than as pets. It's impossible to know how many, if any, talked.

Free ship: a ship on which the pirates get an equal share of any goods they steal

Prize: a captured ship

Piece of eight: a Spanish silver dollar used as currency across the globe

Doubloon: a Spanish gold coin worth four dollars

'I be dreaming of doubloons and pieces of eight!'

Merchantman: a cargo ship

East Indiaman: a merchant ship of the East India Company – sure to be carrying a valuable cargo

Man-of-war: a Royal Navy warship – pirates beware!

'That be no merchantman – it be a man-o-war!'

TALK
LIKE A
PIRATE

In 1995, the American authors and pirate enthusiasts John Baur and Mark Summers inaugurated International Talk Like a Pirate Day, to be marked each year on 19 September. In popular culture, pirates typically talk with a strong West Country accent as if they only came from Cornwall or Devon. Of course, pirates were from all over the place. But the West Country pirate voice can be traced back to Walt Disney's 1950 film adaptation of *Treasure Island*. This was the studio's first live action production, with the Dorset-born actor Robert Newton (1905–56) cast as Long John Silver, a role he repeated twice for cinema and television.

His memorable performance has profoundly influenced the popular perception of what a pirate should sound like. Newton also played, in similar style, the title role in the 1952

Hollywood film *Blackbeard the Pirate*. Without him, it's doubtful that International Talk Like a Pirate Day would exist, relegating 19 September to just another dull day with no opportunity to say 'Aaarrr, me hearties' at will.

FILM FACT

A silent film of Treasure Island *was released in 1920. The American actress Shirley Mason played the character of Jim Hawkins. Davy Jones, of the 1960s pop group and television series 'The Monkees', voiced the character in a 1973 animated version of the story. And in 1990, Christian Bale took on the part of Hawkins, playing opposite Charlton Heston as Long John Silver.*

RULES IS RULES: HOW TO BEHAVE AS A PIRATE

A pirate captain wanted a happy crew and a well-run ship. Achieving this increased the chances of gaining success and wealth. But how did a pirate captain ensure his crew was disciplined and ready to fight? The answer might seem surprising, but many captains introduced a code of behaviour that regulated life on board ship and indicated what the punishments might be for breaking the rules. One of the most famous pirate codes was that of Bartholomew Roberts.*

1. Every man has a vote in deciding important matters; has an equal right to any fresh supplies or strong liquor that are seized, and he may use them at pleasure unless a shortage makes it necessary to introduce rationing for the good of all.

---

* This version has been modernised – not everything written more than 300 years ago still makes sense!

This allowed the crew to choose their captain and live an easier and more comfortable life than in a warship or merchant vessel.

2. Every man to be allowed fairly, in turn, additional goods, like new clothes, from any captured prize. But if they cheat the crew out of anything to the value of a dollar (a piece of eight), they will be punished by marooning. If the robbery is between two individuals, the guilty party will be punished by the slitting of his ears and nose, before being put ashore in a place where he will encounter hardships.

This avoided disputes over who was entitled to what and helped maintain good discipline on board.

3. No person to gamble with cards or dice for money.

Gambling could be a major source of arguments and resentment, which might easily undermine discipline. Banning it removed this danger, making the captain's life much easier.

4. Lights and candles to be put out at eight o'clock at night. If any of the crew wants to continue drinking after that hour, they must do it on the open deck.

This helped to keep sleepy pirates away from their rowdy crewmates, avoiding arguments about bedtime!

5. All members of the crew should keep their pistols and cutlass clean and ready for use.

The crew always needed to be prepared to fight as a prize might be spotted at any moment.

6. No women to be allowed on board. If any man is found to have seduced a woman and taken her to sea in disguise, he will suffer death.

Romance and jealousy could also damage discipline!

7. Any man deserting the ship, or their quarters in a battle, is to be punished with death or marooning.

A ship required a crew, so abandoning it needed to be punished severely to discourage any wider mutiny.

8. No hitting one another when on board ship. Every man's quarrel to be settled on shore with sword and pistol. Those in disagreement are to fight a duel with pistols. If both men miss, they are then to fight with swords. The first to draw blood is the victor.

Pirates were meant to capture prizes rather than fight each other.

9. No man should talk of leaving piracy until each member of the crew has shared £1,000. If any man should lose a limb or become disabled, he is to have 800 pieces of eight, with smaller amounts for lesser injuries.

Financial rewards and compensation were further encouragements to remain with the pirate crew.

10. The captain and quartermaster to receive two shares of any prize; the master, boatswain and gunners one-and-a-half shares, and the other officers one-and-a-quarter shares. All others to receive one share.

The relatively even sharing out of goods and money from a captured prize avoided disputes and encouraged everyone to take part in the action.

11. The musicians to have rest on Sundays, but to play the other six days and nights.

Clearly, entertained pirates were happy pirates, but even the worst musicians need a day off!

HENRY EVERY

Henry Every (sometimes Avery) was one of the most successful pirates of the Western world. He was never captured. In 1695, while in the Indian Ocean, his six pirate ships attacked a Mughal merchant fleet of 25 vessels, many of which were laden with jewels, precious metals and other valuable goods.

Every and his crew seized treasure worth £600,000, the equivalent of more than £100 million today. Each member of the crew got around £1,000 – a very substantial sum at the time. The whereabouts of Every's fortune remains unknown to this day, although claims have been made that it might be buried somewhere in Cornwall.

> BORN: *Newton Ferrers, near Plymouth, England, 1659*
> PIRATE CAREER: *1694–96*
> DIED: *disappeared, date of death unknown*

LESSON 2

....

BUCCANEERING BEHESTS AND BEHAVIOURS, OR HOW TO GIVE PIRATICAL ORDERS AND RESPOND TO THE CAPTAIN'S COMMANDS

Aye: yes

Aye, aye: order understood

Ahoy!: a call to get attention

Sail ho!: a ship has been spotted

> *'Sail ho! Man the guns.'*

Give no quarter: show no mercy in a fight

> *'Give no quarter, men! We'll have this ship no matter the cost.'*

Fire in the hole: a warning given before a gun is fired

Heave to: bring the ship to a stop

Yo-ho-ho: a call to get attention

> '*Fifteen men on the Dead Man's Chest*
> *Yo-ho-ho, and a bottle of rum!*
> *Drink and the devil had done for the rest*
> *Yo-ho-ho, and a bottle of rum!*'

Pirates' song from *Treasure Island*

DEADLY DATA

Pirates didn't make their victims walk the plank. They threw them overboard or left them on deserted islands. In Treasure Island, *Jim Hawkins discovers Ben Gunn, a half-crazed member of Captain Flint's pirate crew. He was abandoned alone on the island for years and developed a craving for cheese, ideally grilled! In real life, the most famous marooned person wasn't a pirate but a privateer. Alexander Selkirk (1676–1721) was put ashore on Más a Tierra, one of the Juan Fernández Islands off the coast of Chile, in 1704, having complained to his captain about the seaworthiness of the ship.* Selkirk was right to be worried, the ship later sank with no survivors. In 1709, after four years and four months entirely alone, he was finally rescued. Selkirk was the inspiration for Daniel Defoe's novel* Robinson Crusoe *(1719).*

---

* The largest of the Juan Fernández Islands is now named Alejandro Selkirk after the famous castaway. The second biggest island, where Selkirk was marooned, is known today as Robinson Crusoe.

CAPTAIN JOHNSON'S PIRATE PHRASES

Much of what we know about pirates comes from Captain Charles Johnson's *A General History of the Robberies and Murders of the most notorious Pyrates*, which was first published in 1724. Captain Johnson is a pseudonym for the real author, so who wrote the book? For many years it was believed to be the author Daniel Defoe (about 1660–1731), but research has now shown that Defoe could not have been the author. Previously, scholars found lots of similarities between phrases in Defoe's writing and that of Johnson, but these were common to many authors. More recently, stylistic inconsistencies have been used to show that the book wasn't penned by Defoe.

Currently, the journalist and printer Nathaniel Mist (d. 1737) seems to be the most likely candidate. He probably used newspaper reports and trial records to weave together the biographical chapters. The book has proved very popular: it remains in print. However, it is not a very reliable source for the history of pirates. Whoever wrote it certainly exaggerated the lives and activities of various pirates to appeal to the reading public. Nevertheless, the book contains many memorable descriptions of pirates and some pithy piratical phrases...

> *'Like their patron the Devil, [pirates] must make mischief their sport, cruelty their delight and damning souls their constant employment.'*

> *'[Pirates] going about like roaring lions, seeking whom they might devour.'*

Bartholomew Roberts:

> 'No, a merry life and a short one, shall be my motto.'

Mary Read:

> 'As to hanging, it is no great hardship. For if it were not for that, every cowardly fellow would turn pirate and so unfit the sea that men of courage would starve.'

Henry Every:

'I am a man of fortune and must seek my fortune.'

Of Charles Vane and his men:

'They shared their booty and spent some time in a riotous manner of living, as is the custom of pirates.'

Just a minute, who on earth is Charles Vane? Vane (about 1680–1721) was a British pirate operating in the Caribbean from 1716–1721. He appears to have been a rather cruel character, who beat up sailors from captured ships. Vane was arrested and sent to trial in Jamaica, where he was sentenced to death on 29 March 1721.

Captain Holford to Charles Vane:

> 'Charles, I shan't trust you aboard my ship unless I [make] you a prisoner; for I shall have you caballing with my men, knock me on the head, and run away with my ship a-pirating.'

And Captain Holford? We don't know much about him, but he was pirating in the 1710s.

Description of Blackbeard:

> 'This beard was black, which he suffered to grow of an extravagant length; as to breadth, it came up to his eyes; he was accustomed to twist it with ribbons, in small tails [...] and turn them about his ears.'

Samuel Bellamy:

> *'I am a free prince, and I have as much authority to make war on the whole world, as he who has a hundred sail of ships at sea, and an army of 100,000 men in the field, and this my conscience tells me.'*

Samuel 'Black Sam' Bellamy (1689–1717) was only a pirate for about a year. Unlike many pirates, he wasn't executed or killed in battle but lost at sea during a violent storm on 26 April 1717.

> *'I scorn to do any one a mischief, when it is not for my advantage.'*

ANNE BONNY AND MARY READ

ANNE BONNY
BORN: *near Cork, Ireland, 1698*
PIRATE CAREER: *1719–20*
DIED: *possibly of natural causes, South Carolina, US, April 1782*

> **MARY READ**
> BORN: *England, about 1695*
> PIRATE CAREER: *1719–20*
> DIED: *in prison, Port Royal, Jamaica, April 1721*

Anne Bonny entered piracy as the lover of John 'Calico Jack' Rackham (d. 1720), a notable pirate operating in the Caribbean. They seized a ship carrying Mary Read, who willingly joined them.

When Rackham's ship was captured, it is said that Bonny and Read were the only ones on board who fought their attackers. Captain Johnson recorded that Read is meant to have exclaimed: 'If there's a man among ye, ye'll come up and fight like the man ye are to be.' He also reported that the last words of Bonny to Rackham in prison were: 'I am sorry to see you here, but if you had fought like a man, you needn't be hanged like a dog.'

RECRUITING WRENS

It should be noted that women couldn't join the Royal Navy until 1917 and the founding of the Women's Royal Naval Service (WRNS), also known as the Wrens. But even then, they only served ashore. Women were recruited to a variety of roles to help free up more men to go to sea. They weren't allowed to serve at sea in the Royal Navy until 1993.

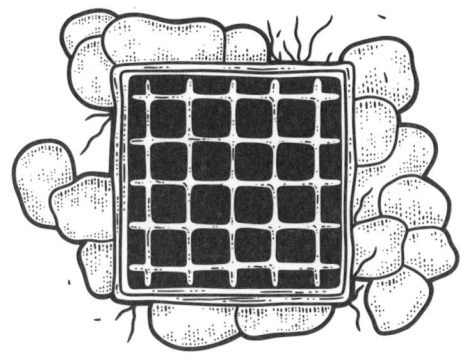

At their trial, Bonny and Read were sentenced to death, but they avoided execution as both were pregnant, or at least claimed to be. Read died of fever in prison in 1721. Bonny may have been released, surviving into old age, but the evidence is inconclusive.

Although Bonny and Read are among the most famous pirates, they were far from the most successful. One contender for that honour is a Chinese pirate.

ZHENG YI SAO, THE ULTIMATE 'MASTER' PIRATE?

> **BORN:** *Xinhui, China, about 1775*
> **PIRATE CAREER:** *1801–10*
> **DIED:** *Nanhai, China, 1844*

Zheng Yi Sao, born Shi Yang, has some claim to being the most successful pirate of all time. In 1801, she married a pirate called Zheng Yi, adopting his name and Sao, meaning 'wife of'. She took over the running of his huge pirate force when he died in 1807. It has been estimated that Zheng commanded 80,000 men and 1,800 vessels of various sizes. She kept her vast force together with harsh discipline: anyone disobeying orders faced beheading. Her fleet, the so-called Red Fleet, was never defeated and she was never caught.

Clever pirates knew when to abandon their life of crime, which is exactly what Zheng achieved. At the height of her power in 1810, she negotiated with the Chinese government to withdraw from piracy and avoid any punishment for her many illegal acts. Zheng died peacefully as a long-retired pirate in 1844 aged about 69, having operated a notorious gambling den in Macao with her second husband. It could be said she swapped pirate ships for poker chips!

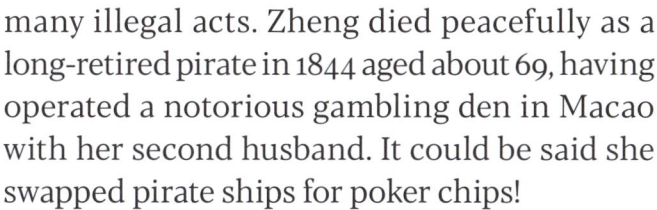

DEMOCRATIC DECISIONS
Some pirates elected their captain and officers. If they didn't capture enough treasure, the crew could vote them out and put someone better in charge. However, during fighting against another ship the captain's word was law.

WHAT DID PIRATES LOOK LIKE?

Pirates didn't have a uniform. They wore everyday, practical clothes. But our idea of what pirates should look like has been heavily influenced by book descriptions and illustrations, and costumes from stage and screen. Captain Johnson's account of the appearance of the notorious pirate Blackbeard is an early example of an author creating an intimidating impression of a pirate: '...in time of action, he wore a sling over his shoulders, with three brace of pistols [that's six!], hanging in holsters like bandoliers; he wore a fur-cap, and stuck a lighted match on each side, under it'. Long John Silver, described some 150 years later in vivid detail by the protagonist of *Treasure Island*, Jim Hawkins, is perhaps the figure who has shaped our image of the pirate like no other: 'I was sure he must be Long John. His left leg was cut close by the hip, and under his left shoulder he carried a crutch, which he managed with wonderful dexterity, hopping upon it like a bird. He was very tall and strong, with a face as big as a ham, plain and pale, but intelligent and smiling.' The appearance of the character Billy Bones, meanwhile, conjures a feeling of violence and danger, with 'hands ragged and scarred' and 'a dirty, livid white' slash from a sabre across his cheek.

The work of American artist and author Howard Pyle (1853–1911, see pages 66 and 71) had a particularly strong impact on later depictions of pirates. Pyle wrote and illustrated a series of pirate stories that were published in various magazines in the late nineteenth century. He developed a distinct style for the look of his pirates that blended elements of baroque, aristocratic fashion with stereotypical examples of Romani dress. The result was colourfully flamboyant with capes, hats, sashes and headscarves. These were largely impractical for any real-life pirate.

While Pyle's illustrations covered all the great pirate myths, with images of buried treasure and men forced to walk the plank, they also dealt with the harsh realities of piracy, like being marooned on a desert island. Pyle didn't limit himself to fictional pirates either, characters like Captain Kidd were reimagined by the artist too. Captain Johnson's description of Bartholomew Roberts before his fatal encounter with Captain Ogle gives a sense of where Howard Pyle got some of his inspiration from:

> *'Roberts himself made a gallant figure [...] dressed in a rich crimson damask waistcoat and breeches, a red feather in his hat, a gold chain round his neck, with a diamond cross hanging to it, a sword in his hand and two pair of pistols hanging at the end of a silk sling, slung over his shoulders (according to the fashion of the pirates)...'*

FINANCIAL FACT

Most pirates shared any treasure fairly among the crew. This meant everyone on board a pirate ship had a reason to fight. Often the captain's share was only twice as large as that of the lowest member of the crew. This was very different to the 'prize money' given out by the Royal Navy for the capture of enemy ships. A naval commander got by far the largest share, making sure he had an incentive to fight, but the ordinary crew got very little for their efforts. However, the pirate system was only fair if they were honest with each other. In A General History of the Pyrates, *Captain Johnson alleged that Henry Every escaped with a huge amount of treasure, cheating his crew out of a vast fortune. This is almost certainly untrue, but how much honour can there have been among a rascally band of sea thieves?*

Pyle's stories were collected into *Howard Pyle's Book of Pirates* by Merle De Vore Johnson and published in 1921. His idiosyncratic take on pirate fashion proved to be the perfect inspiration for fledgling Hollywood costume designers. There is a direct line from his pen to the early appearances of pirates in black-and-white films, through the Technicolor era and down to the digital age of Disney's Jack Sparrow and beyond...

PIRATICAL AND ANTI-PIRATICAL PLACES

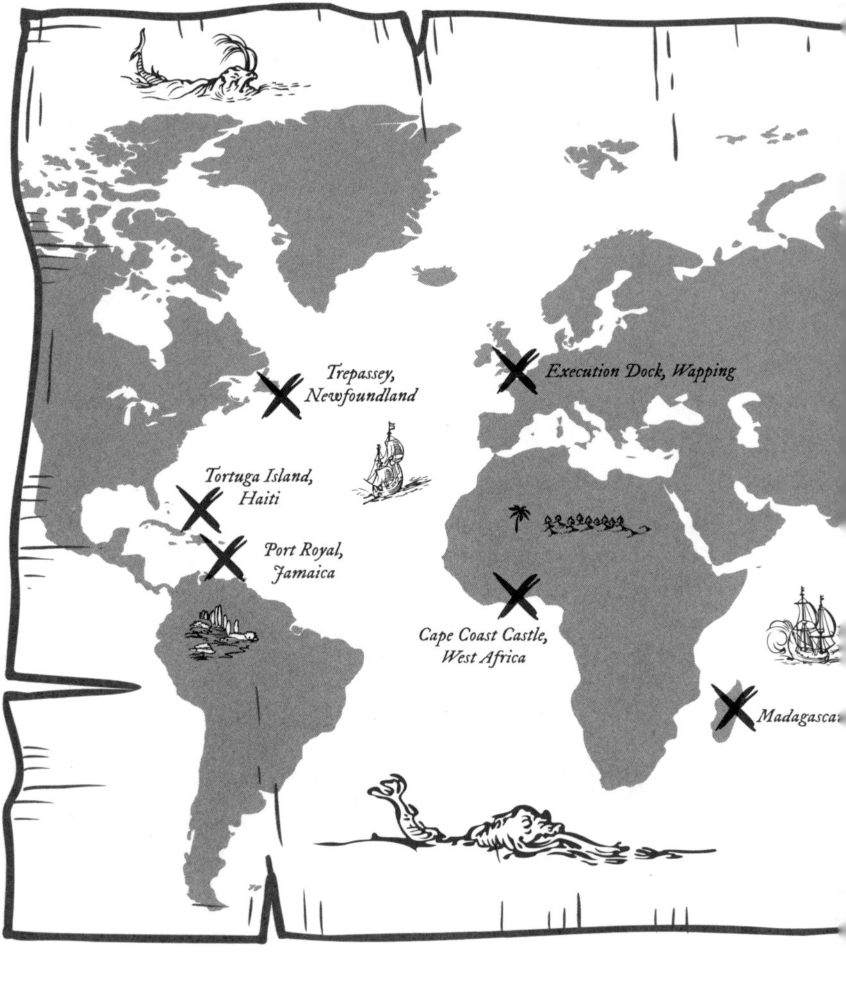

- Trepassey, Newfoundland
- Execution Dock, Wapping
- Tortuga Island, Haiti
- Port Royal, Jamaica
- Cape Coast Castle, West Africa
- Madagascar

Ladrones Islands, China

PIRATE HAUNTS

Pirates roved about on the high seas, moving from shore to shore seeking prizes to plunder. But some places became notorious through their association with piracy...

PORT ROYAL, JAMAICA

Jamaica became an English colony after it was captured from Spain in 1655. Port Royal, on the island's south-east coast, was a base for English privateers in the second half of the seventeenth century. It gave them easy access to Spanish shipping lanes, where they sailed in search of prizes.

Not all privateers stayed within the law, and many became pirates. During the 'golden age', Port Royal gained a reputation as 'the wickedest city on Earth'. Here pirates spent their ill-gotten gains, paying out huge sums on alcohol, women and entertainment.

But Port Royal had other practical reasons for being a good pirate base of operations. It had a safe harbour, protecting shipping during the hurricane season. It also had shallow shores that allowed for the careening of hulls and other essential ship repairs. However, a devastating earthquake on 7 June 1692 left most of the town destroyed and below water. Port Royal's time as a pirate paradise was over.

MADAGASCAR AND THE MYSTERIOUS COLONY OF LIBERTATIA

In the late seventeenth century, the large island of Madagascar off the east coast of Africa became a base for pirates looking to prey on the rich trade of the Indian Ocean. It has also become known for Captain James Misson and the founding of the pirate colony of Libertatia (sometimes Libertalia). According to Captain Johnson, Misson was a French pirate. He established Libertatia to be a democratic utopia, free from rigid authority and discrimination, where pirates and piracy could flourish out of reach of the legal authorities.

There is a problem, however. No evidence has been found to suggest that either Captain Misson or Libertatia ever existed. It appears this pirate colony was as real as Treasure Island or Neverland!

TORTUGA ISLAND, HAITI

Just to the north of present-day Haiti is Tortuga Island, named by Christopher Columbus because its shape resembled that of a turtle shell. English, French and Dutch privateers, also known as buccaneers, made use of Tortuga as a base of operations in the mid-seventeenth century, despite opposition from Spanish forces.

In 1670, the Welsh privateer Henry Morgan invited the Tortuga buccaneers to join him.

The following year, he and a force of about 2,000 buccaneers sailed to Panama, sacking the Spanish settlements there and stealing vast amounts of treasure. This audacious show of buccaneer power was the last great use of Tortuga as a piratical base. France began to take greater control of the island in the 1680s and the pirates moved elsewhere. Pirates always preferred to be ahead of the law!

TREPASSEY, NEWFOUNDLAND, CANADA

On the south-eastern tip of Newfoundland is the small fishing village of Trepassey. This doesn't really sound like a typical pirate haunt, and nor was it. However, on 21 June 1720 it was raided by Bartholomew Roberts, who entered

Buccaneers' Bugle

22 AUGUST 1720 — 1 piece of eight

PROFANE PIRATES PIQUE PUBLIC PRINCIPLES

There was nothing heard among the pirates all the while but cursing, swearing, damning, and blaspheming to the greatest degree imaginable.

From the *Boston News-Letter*, 15–22 August 1720, reporting on Bartholomew Roberts's crew

the harbour with his black flag flying, trumpets blowing and drum beating. Roberts had only one ship but took control of the settlement and its many vessels, with ship captains surrendering to avoid a fight. Captain Johnson's *A General History* provides a much-exaggerated account:

> *'It is impossible particularly to recount the destruction and havoc they made here, burning and sinking all the shipping [...] destroying the fisheries and stages of the poor planters without remorse or compunction [...] They are like mad men that cast firebrands, arrows and death and say, are we not in sport?'**

The inhabitants of Trepassey would not forget Roberts's unwelcome visit.

---

* Fact checking for fake news: no vessels were sunk, and no-one was killed.

LADRONES ISLANDS, CHINA

Many Chinese pirates were based in and around the Ladrones Islands, south-west of Hong Kong, which are now part of what is known as the Wanshan Archipelago. Chinese pirates were sometimes called 'ladrones'. The term came from a Spanish word for a pirate or thief, presumably because of raids on Spain's shipping in the region.

HAUNTING PIRATES

Some places filled pirates with a sense of doom and deadly dread...

EXECUTION DOCK, WAPPING, ENGLAND

For 400 years until 1830, Execution Dock on the River Thames was used as a place for public hangings. The site was chosen near the low-tide mark, which represented the limit of the Admiralty's authority. The Court of Admiralty was responsible for the trial and execution of pirates.

Hanging was a grisly affair during the 'golden age' of piracy. Unlike in the nineteenth century, when the 'drop' was calculated to break the neck – leading to near-instant death – a short rope was used, which left the condemned to strangle slowly to death and could take up to

45 minutes. As they fell unconscious, the spasms of their limbs became known as the 'Marshal's dance', named after the court official, or to 'dance the hempen jig', referencing the rope. The dead body was left hanging in the noose until at least three tides had submerged it.

> **RANSOMED REALITY**
> *Pirates sometimes held the crew and passengers of a captured ship hostage to gain a ransom for their release. In 1809, for example, Chinese pirates captured Richard Glasspoole and six other men from the* Marquis of Ely, *an East India Company ship. After more than 11 weeks as prisoners, a substantial ransom was paid for their release in both cash and goods. Negotiating with the pirates took some time as they haggled over the amount of money and the quality of the items they wanted in exchange for the men. Pirates could be picky!*

On 16 December 1830, George Davis and William Watts became the last men hanged for piracy at Execution Dock following convictions for their part in a mutiny on the ship *Cyprus*, a convict transport vessel.

CAPE COAST CASTLE, WEST AFRICA

The British-run fort at Cape Coast Castle in present-day Ghana was also home to a Court of Admiralty. It was here that the greatest pirate trial of the 'golden age' took place in early 1722. This was of the crew of the Welsh pirate Bartholomew Roberts. Captain Mungo Herdman was the President of Court, or the judge. He sentenced 52 men to death. Of these, 18 were found 'guilty in the highest degree', resulting in the following harsh judgement from Herdman:

> *'Ye and each of you are adjourned and sentenced to be carried back to the place from whence you came, from thence to the place of execution without the gates of this castle, and there within the flood marks to be hanged by the neck 'till ye are dead, dead, dead. And the Lord have mercy upon your souls. After this ye and each of you shall be taken down, and your bodies hung in chains.'*

For those most guilty, this meant their bodies were coated in tar and hung up on public view in a gibbet cage.

LESSON 3

VILLAINOUS VERNACULAR, OR PIRATE SLANG

Hearties: friends

> *'Aar, me hearties – gather round and we'll count the treasure.'*

Booty: stolen goods or treasure

Landlubber: someone not used to life at sea

> *'Look lively you landlubber! We'll make a seaman of you yet.'*

Old salt: an experienced seaman

Saw-bones: a ship's surgeon

Spyglass: a telescope

> *'Be that a ship? Where's me spyglass?'*

The black spot: a piece of paper with a black mark used as a death threat

Hang the jib: frown

Afeard: afraid

Scuttlebutt: gossip

> *'I be hearing mutterings – what's the scuttlebutt, me hearty?'*

Hempen halter: the hangman's noose

The hempen jig: the spasms or 'dance' during hanging

> *'Where be Pirate Pete?'*
> *'The Navy caught him – he'll be dancing the hempen jig soon enough.'*

Jack Ketch: a hangman or executioner

Cabobbled: confused

> *'I be cabobbled, where's all the treasure gone?'*

Blow the gaff: reveal a secret

> *'I be aiming to take the captain's place, don't you blow the gaff!'*

Abbey-lubber: a lazy sailor avoiding work

> *'Stop dawdling, abbey-lubber! I've got me eye on you.'*

Chowder-headed: stupid

> *'You chowder-headed fool, we've run aground!'*

PIRATE
SHIPS

When they captured a ship, pirates might decide to keep the vessel if it was better than their old one. On occasion, pirates may have used a ship for only a few weeks or even a matter of days before making an upgrade. Some pirate captains were able to command a small squadron of ships, increasing their chances of success.

Many pirates renamed the ships they kept, but some thought it was bad luck. Bartholomew Roberts named several of his ships *Royal Revenge*.

DANGEROUS DISCIPLINE
Pirates were not the chaotic and ill-disciplined crews often seen in films. They followed the captain's orders and spent time carefully repairing and maintaining their ships. They wanted them to sail as fast as possible to capture their targets. A slow ship wasn't likely to be a successful pirate vessel.

* Also a possible pirate ship!

In fact, 'revenge' was rather popular, with Blackbeard commanding *Queen Anne's Revenge* and William Kidd captain of the *New York Revenge*. Kidd also had the *Adventure Galley*.

Pirate ships were of all sorts of shapes and sizes, but they needed to be speedy to catch a prize and well-armed to force victims to surrender. Guns would be aimed at the masts and rigging of a victim's ship to bring down the sails, preventing an escape. This tactic also left the ship afloat, which was handy if you wanted to steal the cargo!

THE JOLLY ROGER

Beware the pirate flag known as the Jolly Roger. It's a sign of danger and death. The origins of the flag are shrouded in mystery. But in the late seventeenth and early eighteenth centuries several pirates of the 'golden age' – like Bartholomew Roberts and Edward 'Ned' Low – adopted their own distinct designs, usually a white or red motif on a black background. These flags often featured skulls, crossed bones, skeletons and hourglasses, which all represented mortality.

For pirates, such a flag was a form of visual and psychological weapon. Hauling up the Jolly Roger when alongside a potential prize might be enough to make the ship's crew surrender without a fight. This was ideal for a pirate captain as it meant robbery without the risks of hand-to-hand combat. On occasion, a pirate ship might also carry a red flag. If the black Jolly Roger was insufficient to make a ship surrender, flying a red flag signalled that the pirates would fight to the death to capture their target.

HENRY MORGAN

Henry Morgan was a privateer rather than a pirate, but his activities blurred the lines between the two. In 1671, when privateering, he raided the Spanish settlements in Panama. Unfortunately, this was done without Morgan realising that England and Spain had signed a peace treaty, making his activities technically illegal. Nevertheless, Morgan was knighted and made governor of the English colony of Jamaica.

As Sir Henry, he used the money made from privateering to invest in his plantations in Jamaica, where he produced sugar using the labour of enslaved African men, women and children. He found it hard to resist the rum made locally and eventually drank himself to death.

BORN: *Llanrumney (Llanrhymni), Glamorgan, Wales, about 1635*
PIRATE CAREER: *intermittent, 1660s–70s*
DIED: *Port Maria, Jamaica, 25 August 1688*

PIRATES
IN FICTION

The adventures of historical pirates are full of action, intrigue, deceit, violence and gruesome deaths. But this seems not to be enough for some authors, who've added key elements like treasure maps, walking the plank and even talking parrots to turn the already fantastical into something even more exciting. Others have transformed the bloodthirsty pirates of the past into much more comic and cuddly characters, suitable for readers and viewers of all ages. In the world of fiction, there is, quite literally, a pirate for everybody.

TREASURE ISLAND, ROBERT LOUIS STEVENSON

The origins of Robert Louis Stevenson's tropical pirate adventure *Treasure Island* lay in 1881 with a damp and chilly summer holiday spent near Balmoral in Aberdeenshire. Stevenson and his 13-year-old stepson Lloyd (later known as Sam) amused themselves by drawing a map of a fictitious island, adding place names and other features. Stevenson then wrote in the top right-hand corner the words 'Treasure Island'. This map quickly inspired what was to become his first novel.

The story began life as a series of weekly instalments in the children's magazine *Young Folks*, appearing between October 1881 and January 1882. It was then published in book form in 1883. The novel has proved popular since that day – it has never been out of print.

Stevenson's prose is full of drama and memorable moments. It also introduced many of our ideas of how pirates should behave. The adventure begins with the arrival of the old pirate Billy Bones at the Admiral Benbow Inn, which is run by the parents of Jim Hawkins, the boy hero of the book. Bones starts telling tales of his pirate past: 'His stories were what frightened people worst of all. Dreadful stories they were – about hanging, and walking the plank, and storms at sea, and the Dry Tortugas, and wild deeds and places on the Spanish Main...'

After Bones is killed, Jim describes the treasure map he found among the dead pirate's possessions:

> *'...there fell out the map of an island, with latitude and longitude, soundings, names of hills and bays and inlets, and every particular that would be needed to bring a ship to a safe anchorage upon its shores [...] There were several additions of a later date, but above all, three crosses of red ink – two on the north part of the island, one in the southwest [...] and in a small, neat hand, very different from the captain's tottery characters, these words: "Bulk of the treasure here".'*

Having sailed to the Caribbean, witnessed murder and even killed a man himself, Jim has nightmares about his time on Treasure Island: 'Oxen and wain-ropes would not bring me back again to that accursed island; and the worst dreams that ever I have are when I hear the surf booming about its coasts, or start upright in bed, with the sharp voice of Captain Flint still ringing in my ears: "Pieces of eight! Pieces of eight!".'*

THE PIRATES OF PENZANCE, W.S. GILBERT AND ARTHUR SULLIVAN

William Schwenck (W.S.) Gilbert (1836–1911) and Arthur Sullivan (1842–1900) completed their comic operetta *The Pirates of Penzance* in 1879. It premiered in New York and was a great success on both sides of the Atlantic.

---

* Captain Flint was Long John Silver's talking parrot.

It is still performed regularly by professional and amateur companies.

Rather than the tropical islands of the Caribbean, the story centres on the Cornish coast at Penzance. It's not the Royal Navy that is hunting the pirates but the local constabulary. The plot concerns the pirate apprentice Frederic, who is about to celebrate his 21st birthday and coming of age. This will allow him to finish his apprenticeship, leave the pirates and marry his sweetheart, Mabel. But Frederic learns that he was born on 29 February, meaning he has not seen 21 birthdays, but only five. It is

soon calculated that he will be apprenticed to the pirates until he's 84! The plot twists in every imaginable direction until, thanks to some unexpected and typically 'topsy-turvy' revelations (no spoilers here!), Frederic can finally wed.

> *'Oh, better far to live and die*
> *Under the brave black flag I fly [...]*
>
> *For I am a Pirate King!*
> *And it is, it is a glorious thing*
> *To be a Pirate King!'*

'Oh, better far to live and die',
Pirate King and Pirates' chorus
from *The Pirates of Penzance*

PETER PAN, J.M. BARRIE

James Matthew Barrie (1860–1937) wrote *Peter Pan, or the boy who wouldn't grow up* as a play. It was first performed at the Duke of York's

Theatre in London on 27 December 1904. Largely set in Neverland and filled with theatrical effects and magical adventure, it proved an immediate hit. At the centre of the plot is Peter Pan's arch-enemy, the sinister James Hook, the pirate captain of the *Jolly Roger*:

> *'Cruellest jewel in that dark setting is Hook himself [...] his hair dressed in long curls which look like black candles about to melt, his eyes blue as forget-me-not and of profound insensibility, save when he claws, at which time a red spot appears in them. He has an iron hook instead of a right hand, and it is with this he claws. He is never more sinister than when he is most polite [...] This courtliness impresses even his victims on the high seas, who note that he always says "Sorry" when prodding them along the plank.'*

This polite, Eton-educated villain was played by the English actor Gerald du Maurier (1873–1934) in the premiere. A critic from *The Manchester Guardian* thought he 'shone marvellously' in the role. Du Maurier's daughter Daphne, a noted author, later remembered his characterisation of Hook: 'How he was hated, with his flourish, his poses, his dreaded diabolical style [...] a tragic and rather ghastly creation that knew no peace [...] a bogey of fear who lives in the grey recesses of every small boy's mind.' Barrie later expanded the play into the 1911 novel *Peter and Wendy*.

PETER PAN ON SCREEN
(A *VERY* SELECT SELECTION)

Like *Treasure Island*, *Peter Pan* was ideal for translation onto the big screen. Paramount Studios released a silent, black-and-white film in 1924. At 6 foot 4 inches (1.93m) tall, the Scottish actor Ernest Torrence (1878–1933) made an imposing Captain Hook. Following stage tradition, the American actress Betty Bronson (1906–71) played the eternally youthful Peter.

In 1953, Walt Disney produced a full-length animated film of *Peter Pan* with Captain Hook as a pantomime-style villain *par excellence*. The film also followed stage convention by having the American actor Hans Conried (1917–82) provide the voice of both Hook and Mr Darling, the children's father. Another American actor, Bobby Driscoll (1937–68), voiced Peter. Driscoll had previously played Jim Hawkins in Disney's live-action *Treasure Island* in 1950.

THE SWASHBUCKLING NOVELS OF RAFAEL SABATINI

The Italian-born British author Rafael Sabatini (1875–1950) wrote several highly successful pirate adventure novels in the first half of the twentieth century. These included *The Sea Hawk* (1915), *Captain Blood* (1922), *The Chronicles of Captain Blood* (1931), *The Black Swan* (1932) and *The Fortunes of Captain Blood* (1936). Sabatini's books coincided with the dawn of Hollywood and the movie industry. Many were adapted for the big screen.

The Sea Hawk (1924) was a silent film directed by Frank Lloyd. It cost $800,000 to produce (more than £10 million today) but made $2 million at the box office. Another film of the same name was released in 1940 and starred Errol Flynn, but the plot was entirely different to Sabatini's novel.

Also starring Errol Flynn, as well as Olivia de Havilland and Basil Rathbone, *Captain Blood* (1935) was a black-and-white talkie directed by Michael Curtiz. It's a classic swashbuckling adventure and launched the careers of both

> ### JUST A MINUTE, WHAT DOES SWASHBUCKLING MEAN?
> *Do you swash a buckle, or buckle your swash? Well, a 'swashbuckler' is a swaggering or daredevil adventurer. Therefore, swashbuckling means to behave in such a manner, whether in real-life or on stage and screen. But where does the term come from? Its origins lie in 'swash', meaning the sound of a sword hitting a shield, which can be called a 'buckler'. Put the two together and it all makes sense, doesn't it? In terms of fiction – whether on the page, the stage, or the screen – a swashbuckler will have plenty of sword fights, action and just enough romance.*

Flynn and de Havilland. Some of the battle scenes from *The Sea Hawk* were reused in the movie.

The Technicolor movie *The Black Swan* (1942) was directed by Henry King. Its stars were Tyrone Power and Maureen O'Hara. In her autobiography, O'Hara recalled it was 'everything you could want in a lavish pirate picture: a magnificent ship with thundering cannons [and] a dashing hero battling menacing villains'.

> *'Just because you are caught between the devil and the deep blue sea, that is no reason why you should align yourself with the devil.'*
>
> From *Captain Blood* (1935)

JOHN RYAN AND CAPTAIN HORATIO PUGWASH

The artist and writer John Ryan (1921–2009) created the character of Captain Horatio Pugwash, a pompous but rather inept and cowardly pirate. In 1950, he appeared in cartoon-strip form in the first 19 issues of the *Eagle* comic and later in the *Radio Times*. The stories are aimed at young children and feature Pugwash and the crew of the *Black Pig* in a series of often hapless but humorous adventures.

Between 1957 and 1966, 58 black-and-white television episodes were made using simple, hand-animated figures, which were operated while being broadcast live. Pugwash appeared again on television in colour animation from 1974 to 1975, with regular repeats. A new series aired in 1998. His adventures also continued in various children's books.

Aside from Pugwash, the main characters were Master Mate, Barnabas, Willy and Tom, the cabin boy, whose common sense and bravery usually saved the day. Their arch-enemy was Cut-Throat Jake, a much more successful but far less kindly pirate than Captain Pugwash.

Pugwash had a wide range of pithy and alliterative exclamations:

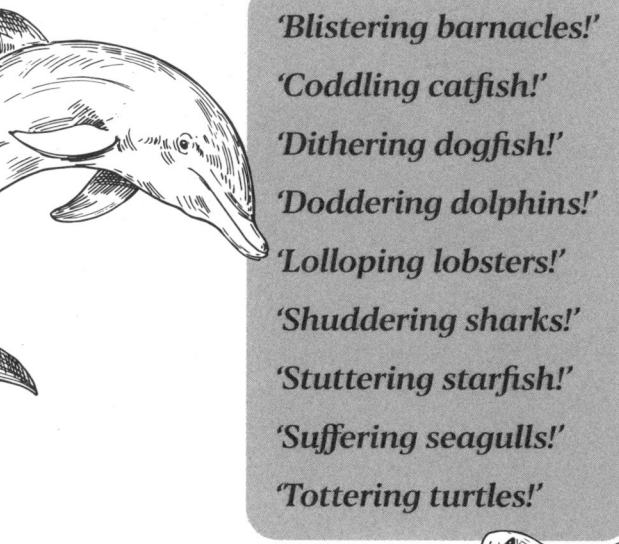

'Blistering barnacles!'
'Coddling catfish!'
'Dithering dogfish!'
'Doddering dolphins!'
'Lolloping lobsters!'
'Shuddering sharks!'
'Stuttering starfish!'
'Suffering seagulls!'
'Tottering turtles!'

PIRATES OF THE CARIBBEAN

The cinema sensation *Pirates of the Caribbean* was inspired by a theme park ride, which opened at Disneyland in Anaheim, California in 1967. It had all the features of a classic pirate adventure – shipwrecks, treasure maps, skeletons and plenty of fighting. The attraction proved hugely popular and can now be found at many of the Disney resorts. Today, the films influence the character and appearance of the ride rather than the other way round.

The idea of loosely adapting elements of the ride and re-imagining them for the big screen proved a lucrative one. There have been five *Pirates of the Caribbean* films: *The Curse of the Black Pearl* (2003), *Dead Man's Chest* (2006), *At World's End* (2007), *On Stranger Tides* (2011) and *Dead Men Tell No Tales* (2017), which was released in some countries as *Salazar's Revenge*.

Together these films have taken more than $4.5 billion (over £3.4 billion) at the box office. This means that they earned more than $100,000 (about £75,000) for every second of screen time!

CAPTAIN JACK SPARROW'S 'BLACK PEARLS' OF WISDOM

The success of the *Pirates of the Caribbean* films has made Captain Jack Sparrow one of the most instantly recognised pirates in fiction or fact. The character survives more by his wits than through brute force and is more likely to flee from a fight than face down his foe, although, ultimately, he always must. Frequently placed in impossible (and, it must be said, implausible) situations and battling against improbable odds, Jack Sparrow has uttered some memorable lines...

> *'I'm dishonest, and a dishonest man you can always trust to be dishonest.'*

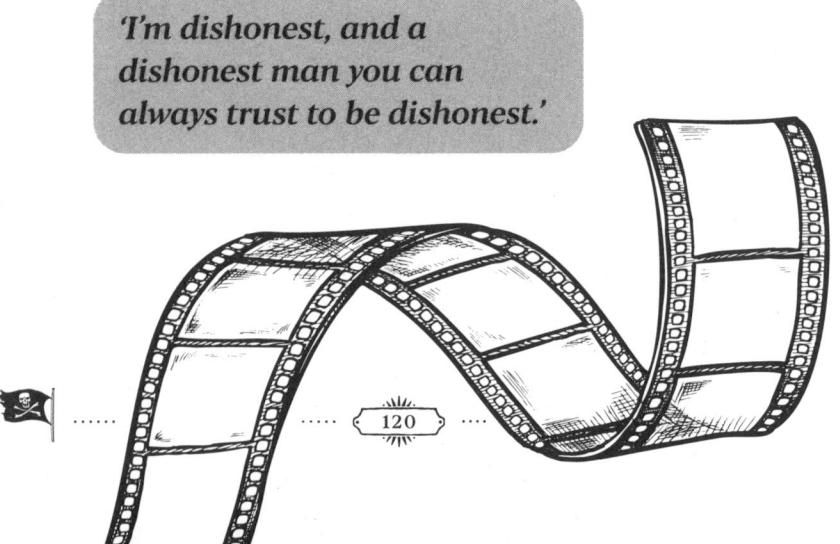

'Why fight when you can negotiate?'

'No survivors? Then where do the stories come from, I wonder?'

'Nobody move! I've dropped me brain!'

'Why is the rum always gone?'

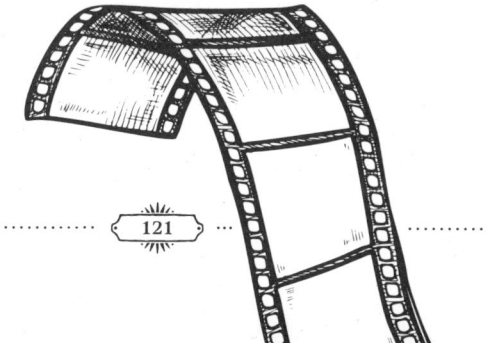

EDWARD TEACH, 'BLACKBEARD'

Blackbeard created an image of terror and violence. He even placed lit, slow-burning fuses in his beard to enhance his fearsome appearance and bloodthirsty reputation.* Captain Johnson noted that 'his eyes, naturally looking fierce and wild, made him [...] look more frightful'.

> BORN: *probably Bristol, England, about 1680*
> PIRATE CAREER: *1716–18*
> DIED: *killed in battle, 22 November 1718*

---

* Although the cynical among us might ask whether they were there simply to ward off the nasty nips of mosquitoes!

In his short pirate career, Blackbeard proved very successful, capturing ships in the Caribbean and along the east coast of North America. In November 1718, Lieutenant Robert Maynard, commanding the Royal Navy warship *Pearl*, engaged him in battle. After fierce fighting, Blackbeard was beheaded. For many years, his severed head was visible on a stake at Chesapeake Bay in Virginia.

Corsairs' Chronicle

3 MARCH 1719 — 1 piece of eight

BEEFY BLOKE BEHEADS BLACKBEARD

[A 'Highlander'] who gave Teach [Blackbeard] a cut on the neck, Teach saying well done lad, the Highlander replied, if it not be well done, I'll do it better, with that he gave him a second stoke, which cut off his head, laying it flat on his shoulder.

From *The Boston News-Letter*, 23 February–3 March 1719

STEDE BONNET, THE 'GENTLEMAN PIRATE'

> BORN: *Bridgetown, Barbados, about 1688*
> PIRATE CAREER: *1717–18*
> DIED: *hanged, Charles Town, South Carolina, US, 10 December 1718*

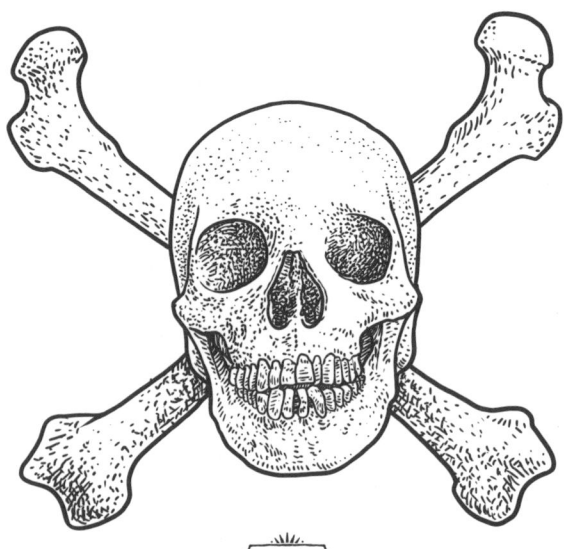

Stede Bonnet was born into a relatively wealthy plantation-owning family. Despite having no seafaring experience, he decided to become a pirate. Some people think he wanted to get away from his unhappy marriage. Bonnet had a local boatyard build him a 10-gun vessel which he named the *Revenge*, a favourite choice among pirates. He then hired a paid crew to sail his ship. He had some success as a pirate, presumably largely a result of the skills of the crew. That said, Bonnet did have military experience, so he was no stranger to fighting.

After various adventures and injuries, Bonnet's luck ran out. He was captured by government forces and sentenced to death. His career may not have been the most illustrious of piracy's 'golden age', but Bonnet's social background and entry into the pirate world have marked him out as rather different to the norm.

WAS FRANCIS DRAKE A PIRATE?

It depends on who you ask! Between December 1577 and September 1580, Francis Drake (about 1540–96) sailed around the world, known as a circumnavigation, in what has been called Drake's Raiding Expedition. During the epic voyage, his ships captured and plundered 13 Spanish vessels, wrecked 12 others, and he also raided some of Spain's overseas settlements. He famously robbed two Spanish treasure ships off the west coast of South America, capturing silver and other valuables worth around £500 million today.

All of this was done by Drake as a privateer, with a royal licence to intercept Spanish ships and disrupt their trade. In other words, under English law, Drake was not a pirate. Drake returned to England with the enormous fortune packed into his ship, the *Golden Hind*. Much of it was used to pay off the national debt. Those who privately invested in the venture made a vast return of around 5,000 per cent.

Drake was granted a knighthood by Queen Elizabeth I. It is commonly thought that Elizabeth dubbed Drake with the royal sword to become Sir Francis on board the *Golden Hind* at Deptford on 4 April 1581. In fact, the ceremony was carried out by a French diplomat, Monsieur de Marchaumont. The Queen was playing politics. The French envoy was trying to negotiate Elizabeth's marriage to the Duke of Anjou, the brother of the French King. By implicating France in the knighting of Drake, Elizabeth gained tacit French acceptance of his actions against Spain, helping her diplomacy.

Drake was now a wealthy man, and his successes made him an English national hero. But the Spanish regarded him as nothing but a despicable pirate and a common criminal. They named him 'El Draco', the dragon.

CHRISTOPHER MYNGS AND THE ART OF GETTING AWAY WITH IT

Christopher Myngs (1625–66) commanded a Royal Navy squadron based in Jamaica. He was ordered to raid Spanish settlements as part of Oliver Cromwell's (1599–1658) actions against Spain. In 1659, Myngs seized silver and other valuables worth more than £300,000, or at least £60 million today.

When he returned to Jamaica to hand over the vast treasure to the English authorities, the chests were found to be empty.

How on earth had that happened? It seems that Myngs and his crew simply stole a fortune. Astonishingly, and despite complaints – not least from the Spanish government – they went unpunished. Little wonder he was one of the more popular commanders in the Royal Navy!

LESSON 4

SHIPBOARD SPEECH, OR MAKING SENSE OF PIRATES AFLOAT

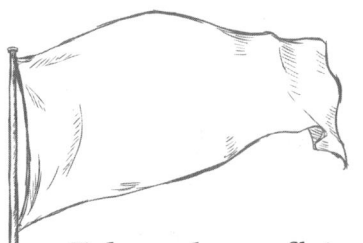

False colours: flying a flag that makes a ship think you're friendly before attacking it

Careen: scrape barnacles and seaweed off the ship's hull to make it sail faster

> *'Get careening, me hearties. This tub be sailing like a haystack!'*

Maroon: abandon a victim on a deserted island

> *'We marooned him on the beach with nothing but a bottle of rum and a loaded pistol for company.'*

Gun: a cannon

Foul bottom: a ship with barnacles and seaweed covering the lower hull

> *'We be sailing slow. A foul bottom, methinks. Time for careening.'*

Sharp bottom: a fast-sailing ship – ideal for a pirate!

> *'We'll keep this ship – it be sharp bottomed!'*

Hands: the crew of a ship

> *'All hands on deck, we're about to board.'*

League: a distance of 3 nautical miles (about 5km)

Fathom: a depth of 6 feet (almost 2m)

Bumboat: a small vessel used to take supplies for sale to a ship at anchor

Barking iron: a large pistol

'Stand back! Me barking iron's loaded and I be ready to shoot.'

Strike colours: lower your ship's flag as a sign of surrender

'Prepare to fire! We'll make him strike his colours.'

Black jack: a leather drinking tankard

'I be thirsty. Fetch me a black jack of ale.'

Piratical Post

24 SEPTEMBER 1717 — 1 piece of eight

BOOZY BUCCANEERS BEWARE!

The pirates [...] entertained themselves so plentifully with madeira wine, that they all got drunk; and the pirate-ship ran aground on a shoal in a place called Nossett's Bay [...] On board of her were 120 men, of whom only two were saved.

From *The London Gazette*, 21–24 September 1717

DRUNKEN DETAILS

Like many pirates, Bartholomew Roberts's crew often celebrated a success by drinking lots of rum and wine. Roberts himself avoided alcohol, preferring a cup of tea instead. Perhaps his desire to keep a clear head helped him to become a highly successful pirate. He captured about 400 vessels of various sizes in his short career.

Gob-stick: a wooden spoon

Cackle fruit: eggs

> *'I be hungry – get some cackle fruit and find me gob-stick.'*

Addle: bad drinking water

Victuals: food or provisions

Hardtack: a ship's biscuit made of flour and water – not very tasty!

> *'Hardtack for dinner? Get me some decent victuals.'*

PIRATE TREASURE (NOT BURIED)

....

A rich cargo that was easy to steal was the ideal prize for any pirate. Jewels and precious metal in the form of coins and bullion were the stuff of pirate dreams, but treasure wasn't always gold and silver. Pirates also stole things they needed like food, gunpowder, cloth and rope. The passengers and crew of captured ships were also targeted. Personal possessions and money were stolen. In some cases, individuals or a whole ship could be held for ransom.

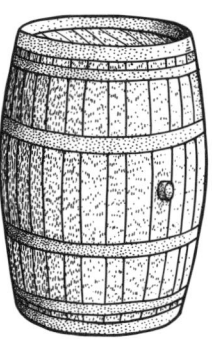

In 1720, Bartholomew Roberts attacked a ship called the *Samuel*. In typical style, Captain Johnson, in his *General History*, described the action as the pirates swarmed aboard: 'They tore up the hatches and entered the hold like a parcel of furies, and with axes and cutlasses, cut and broke open all the bales, cases, and boxes, they could lay their hands on [...] all this was done with incessant cursing and swearing, more like fiends than men.'

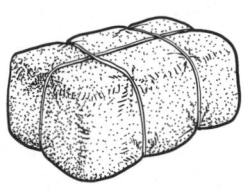

BLACK CAESAR

> BORN: *date and location unknown*
> PIRATE CAREER: *active 1718*
> DIED: *possibly hanged, Williamsburg, Virginia, US, 1719*

Little is known for certain about Black Caesar. He may have been a West African king, who escaped enslavement and became a pirate. He definitely later joined Blackbeard's crew, which included a significant number of Black men. At one point, his crew of 100 included 60 men of African heritage.

During the battle that killed Blackbeard, one of his crew was ordered to blow up the ship. Although he failed, some have identified him as a man called 'Caesar'. He was captured and hanged in 1719. It is not clear, however, whether this man was Black Caesar.

EDWARD 'NED' LOW

BORN: *London, England, about 1690*
PIRATE CAREER: *1721–24*
DIED: *date and location unknown*

Edward 'Ned' Low was a very nasty pirate and involved in crime from childhood. He cruelly wounded and tortured some of his victims by cutting off their ears, lips or noses. He once burnt alive a French cook, telling him: 'You are a greasy fellow, so you'll fry well.' He mainly operated off the east coast of North America, but also plundered shipping in the Caribbean. The fate of Ned Low remains a mystery. After about three years as a pirate, he seems to have disappeared in 1724. Some people think he lived out the rest of his life in Brazil. We may never know...

But Captain Johnson took a very dim view of Low and his cruelties. He concluded the chapter on him with the words: 'the best information we could receive, would be, that he and all his crew were at the bottom of the sea'. Even among pirates, Low plumbed the depths of human behaviour. Perhaps he was the lowest of the Lows.

PIRATE PARDONS

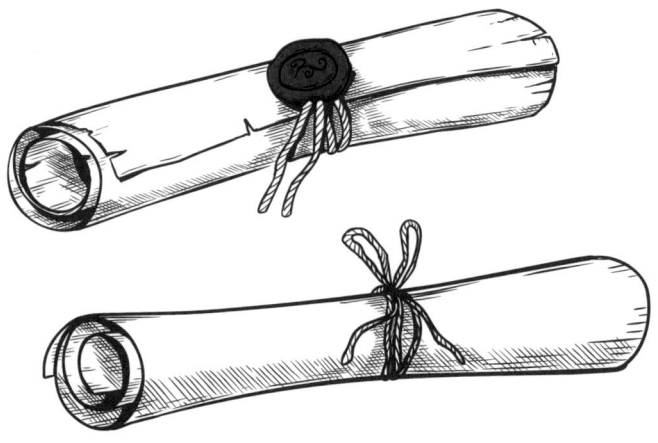

A pirate pardon isn't what a piratical fellow does after burping at the table. (Please note, polite pirates should always say 'excuse me' in such a situation unless they want to get a reputation as a rude and rascally ruffian.) Pardons were offered by the government to persuade pirates to give up piracy and retire as law-abiding citizens. If a pirate agreed to a pardon, the government promised not to prosecute them for past misdeeds provided, of course, they abandoned their lives of crime on the high seas. Many pirates accepted a pardon as a risk-free means of cashing in on their gains. But some simply couldn't resist the lure of the life piratical and the potential of capturing just one more prize. If you broke your pardon and were caught, the punishment was death. Some pirates, like Henry Every and William Kidd, were so notorious that they were denied pardons.

Piratical Post

5 JULY 1725 — 1 piece of eight

REGRETTABLE ROBBERIES RUIN ROB

'Brother sailors, if ever it should be your hard fortune to be taken by the pirates, suffer yourselves to be shot, rather than join with them in their villainy, which has been the cause of my ruin. I forgive all the world, and God forgive me.'

From *Parker's Penny Post*, 5 July 1725, reporting the last words of the Scottish pirate Alexander Rob.

Not much is known about Rob. He was part of the crew of Captain John Gow (about 1698–1725), a piratical Scotsman who was hanged with Rob at Execution Dock in London on 11 June 1725.

FEARSOME FACT

Few pirates enjoyed a long piratical career roving and robbing on the high seas before resting up in genteel retirement. A clever pirate wanted to steal lots of valuables as quickly as possible before returning to ordinary life with plenty of money. The reason for this was simple: being a pirate was very dangerous. You might be hurt or killed in battle. If caught, you faced the death penalty. Bartholomew Roberts was killed in action when gunfire tore out his throat. Blackbeard lost his head (quite literally!) in battle and Captain Kidd was slowly hanged to death. And violent ends aren't just for historical pirates. In Treasure Island, *Jim Hawkins kills the murderous pirate Israel Hands: 'One more step, Mr Hands [...] and I'll blow your brains out. Dead men don't bite, you know.'*

RISK ANALYSIS: WOULD YOU BECOME A PIRATE?

Becoming a pirate wasn't an easy decision to make. If found guilty the punishment was severe. But being a pirate offered the chance of making a fortune – the sort of money that honest work could never provide. Would you 'go on account' and become a pirate, or remain a law-abiding, but poorly paid citizen?

Do you have plenty of money?

- **Aye** → *There's no need for you to become a pirate.*
- **Nay** → *Are you prepared to break the law?*
  - **Aye** → *Are you ready for a life of danger on the high seas?*
    - **Aye** → *Are you prepared to hunt for treasure even if it means death?*
      - **Aye** → *Yo ho ho, me hearty! Now steal a ship, find a crew and off you go a-pirating...*
      - **Nay** → *You be afeard! A pirate life is not for you. Think again about your criminal career.*
    - **Nay** → *Landlubber! Perhaps you're more suited to being a highwayman.*
  - **Nay** → *Crime is not for you. Go home and think of another 'get rich quick' scheme.*

PERCHANCE IT PLEASES, A PLETHORA OF PITHY AND PRACTICAL PIRATICAL PUBLICATIONS TO PERUSE PEACEFULLY AND PROFITABLY IN PURSUANCE OF PLENTIFUL AND PLAYFULLY PERTINENT PARTICULARS; OR, IN OTHER WORDS...

FURTHER READING

David Cordingly and John Falconer, *Pirates: Fact and Fiction*, National Maritime Museum, London, 2021.
Separates what we think is true from what is not, with lots of colourful illustrations.

Terry Deary, *Horrible Histories: Pirates*, Scholastic, New York, 2022.
Full of frightful facts and devilish details.

Captain Charles Johnson, *A General History of the Robberies and Murders of the Most Notorious Pyrates*, Charles Rivington, London, 1724.
There are many editions.

Peter T. Leeson, *The Invisible Hook: The Hidden Economics of Pirates*, Princeton University Press, New Jersey, 2009.
'Blows the gaff' on why pirates behaved the way they did for financial gain.

Neil Rennie, *Treasure Neverland: Real and Imaginary Pirates*, Oxford University Press, Oxford, 2013.
Leaves no pirate myth unbusted!

Rebecca Simon, *The Pirates' Code: Laws and Life Aboard Ship*, Reaktion Books, London, 2023.
An indispensable guide for anyone planning a pleasure cruise on a pirate ship.

A FINAL THOUGHT...

In his poem An Essay on Criticism *(1711), Alexander Pope famously wrote 'To err is human, to forgive, divine.' But surely for this book, we must conclude that 'To err is human, to aar is pirate!'*